the twilight saga

new moon

THE SCORE
MUSIC BY ALEXANDRE DESPLAT

SUMMIT ENTERTAINMENT PRESENTS "THE TWILIGHT SAGA: NEW MOON"
A TEMPLE HILL PRODUCTION IN ASSOCIATION WITH MAVERICK/IMPRINT AND SUNSWEPT ENTERTAINMENT KRISTEN STEWART ROBERT PATTINSON TAYLOR LAUTNER ASHLEY GREENE RACHELLE LEFEVRE BILLY BURKE PETER FACINELLI ELIZABETH REASER NIKKI REED KELLAN LUTZ JACKSON RATHBONE ANNA KENDRICK WITH MICHAEL SHEEN AND DAKOTA FANNING CASTING BY JOSEPH MIDDLETON, C.S.A. MUSIC BY ALEXANDRE DESPLAT MUSIC SUPERVISOR ALEXANDRA PATSAVAS COSTUME DESIGNER TISH MONAGHAN EDITOR PETER LAMBERT PRODUCTION DESIGNER DAVID BRISBIN DIRECTOR OF PHOTOGRAPHY JAVIER AGUIRRESAROBE CO-PRODUCER BILL BANNERMAN EXECUTIVE PRODUCERS MARTY BOWEN GREG MOORADIAN MARK MORGAN GUY OSEARY PRODUCED BY WYCK GODFREY KAREN ROSENFELT BASED ON THE NOVEL "NEW MOON" BY STEPHENIE MEYER

PG-13 PARENTS STRONGLY CAUTIONED
Some Material May Be Inappropriate for Children Under 13
Some Violence and Action

11.20.09

SCREENPLAY BY MELISSA ROSENBERG DIRECTED BY CHRIS WEITZ

Original Motion Picture Soundtrack Available On Atlantic Records

www.newmoonthemovie.com

ISBN 978-1-4234-9062-3

HAL•LEONARD®
CORPORATION
7777 W. BLUEMOUND RD. P.O. BOX 13819 MILWAUKEE, WI 53213

In Australia Contact:
Hal Leonard Australia Pty. Ltd.
4 Lentara Court
Cheltenham, Victoria, 3192 Australia
Email: ausadmin@halleonard.com.au

Visit Hal Leonard Online at
www.halleonard.com

NEW MOON

Composed by ALEXANDRE DESPLAT

ROMEO & JULIET

Composed by ALEXANDRE DESPLAT

Moderately slow

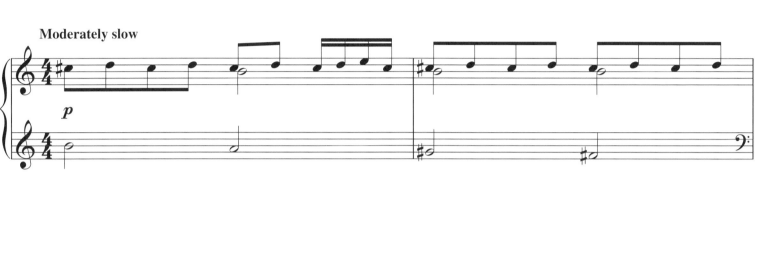

VOLTURI WALTZ

Composed by ALEXANDRE DESPLAT

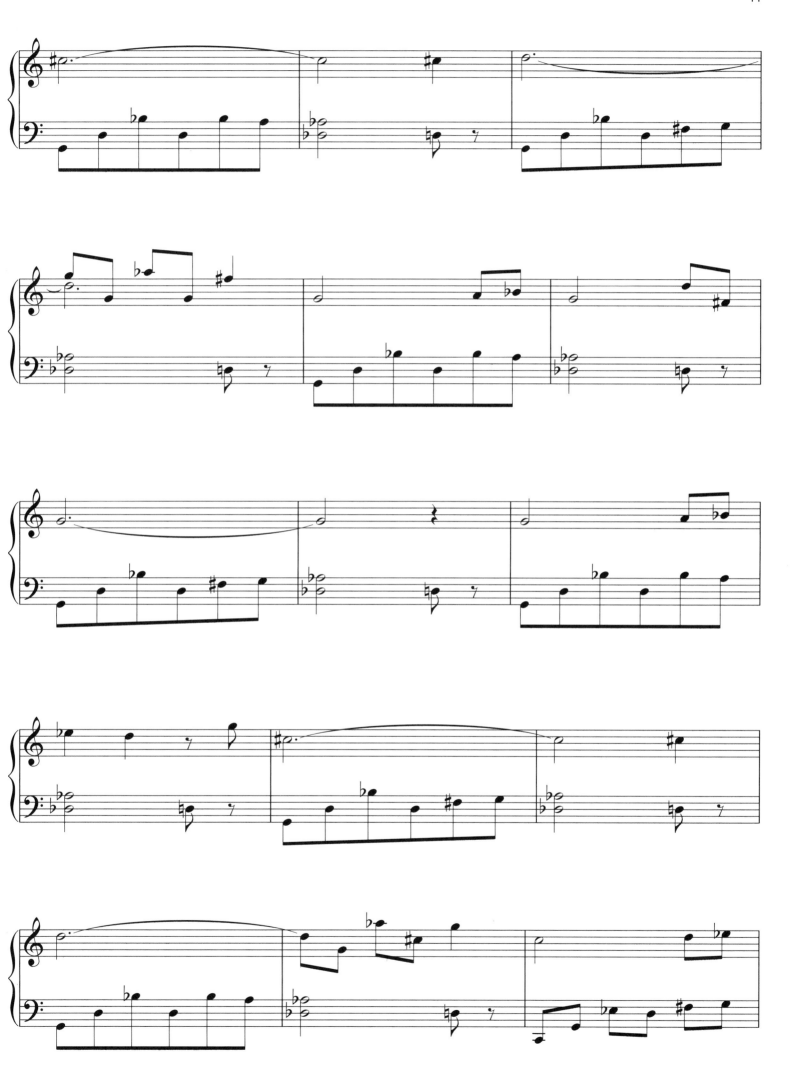

EDWARD LEAVES

Composed by ALEXANDRE DESPLAT

Moderately slow, expressively

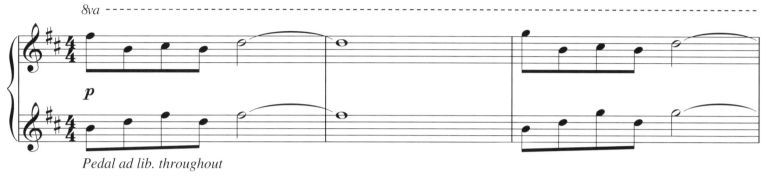

Pedal ad lib. throughout

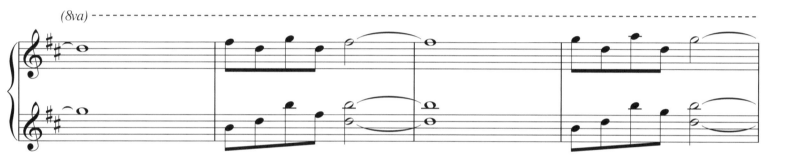

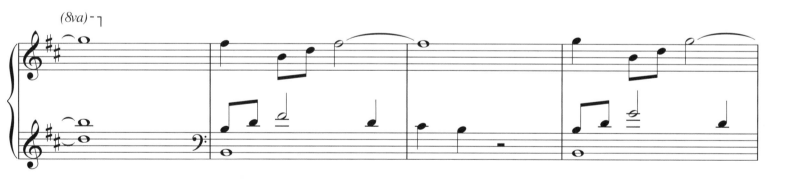

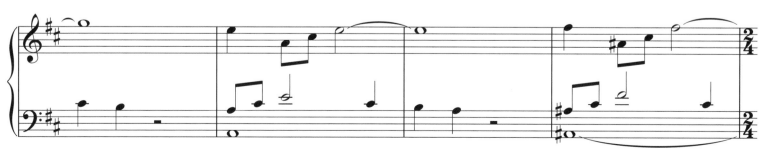

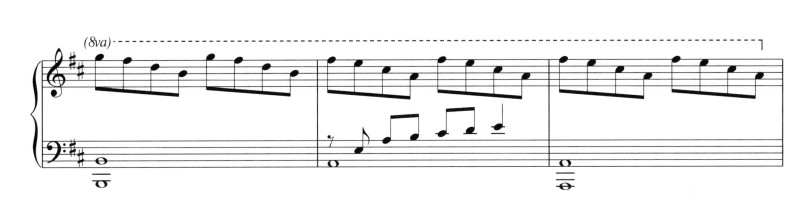

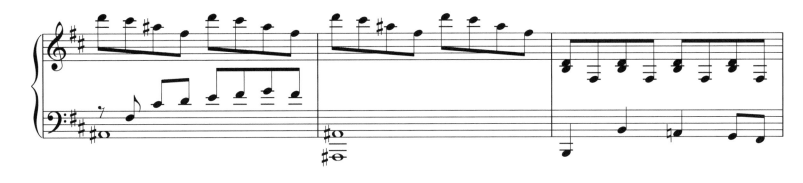

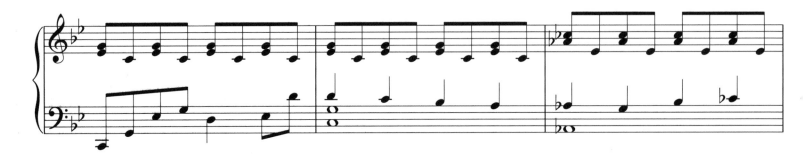

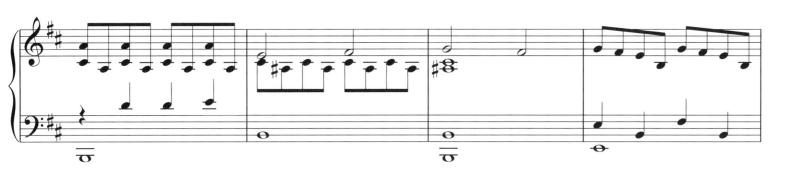

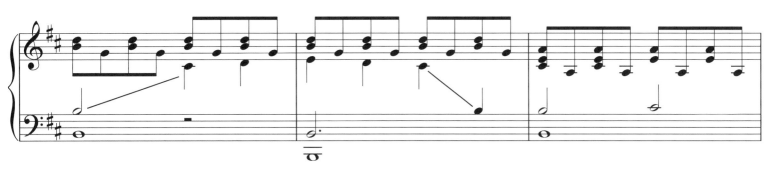

I NEED YOU

Composed by ALEXANDRE DESPLAT

Moderately slow

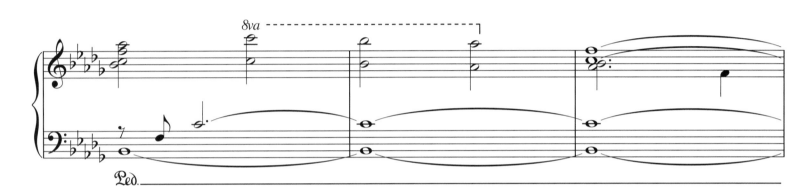

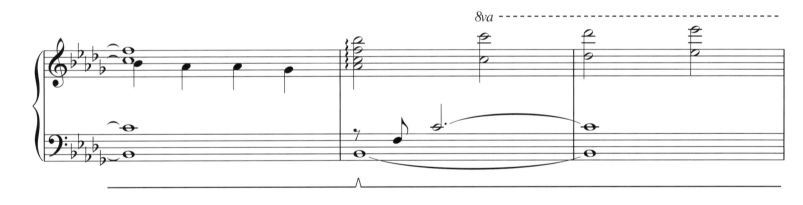

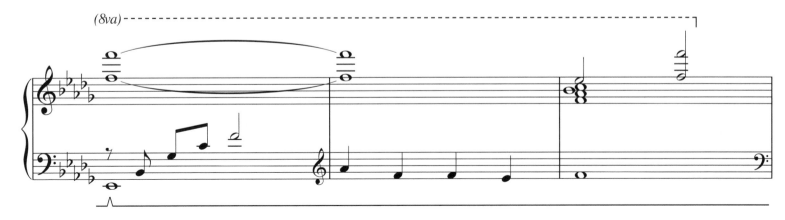

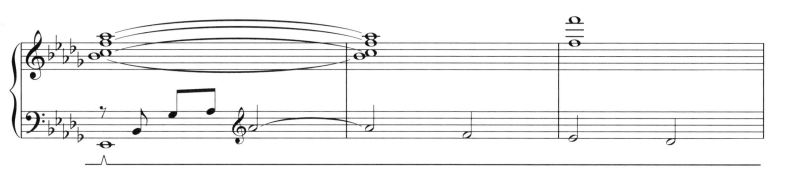

Pedal ad lib. to end

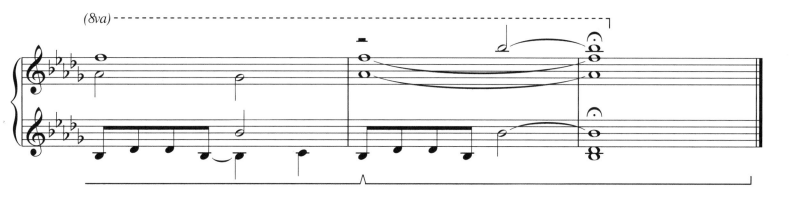

MEMORIES OF EDWARD

Composed by ALEXANDRE DESPLAT

Moderately

Pedal ad lib. throughout

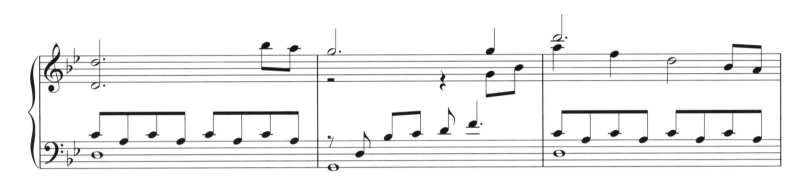

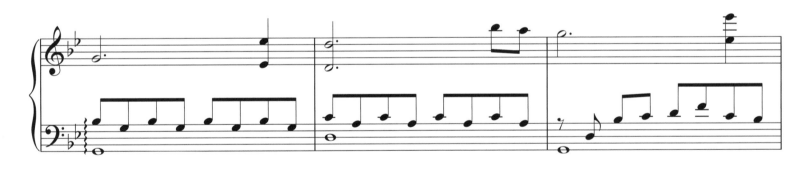

ALMOST A KISS

Composed by ALEXANDRE DESPLAT

Moderately slow

Pedal ad lib. throughout

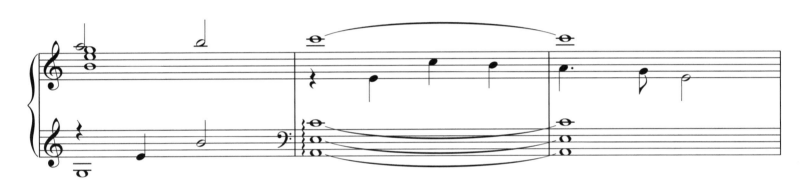

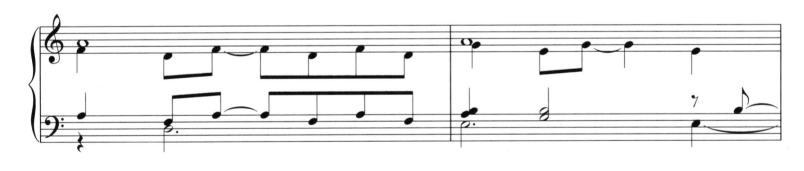

ADRENALINE

Composed by ALEXANDRE DESPLAT

Moderately

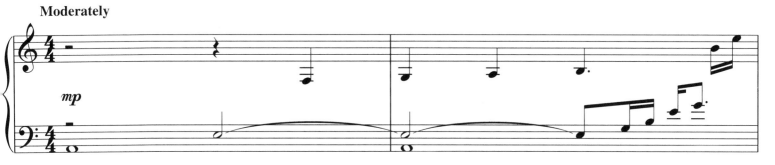

Pedal ad lib. throughout

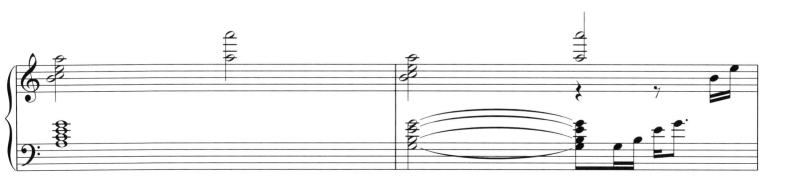

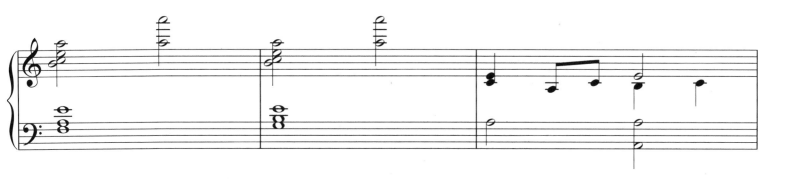

(Pedal ad lib.)

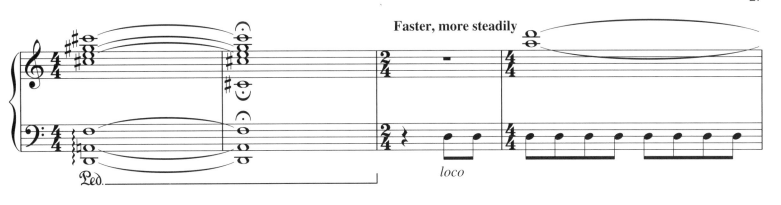

Faster, more steadily

loco

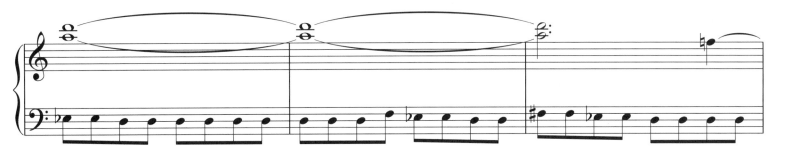

DREAMCATCHER

Composed by ALEXANDRE DESPLAT

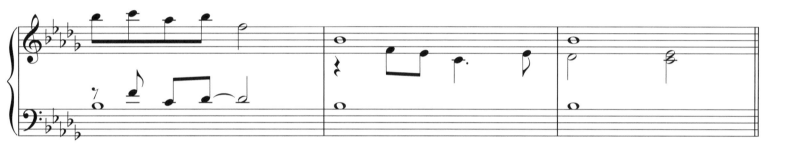

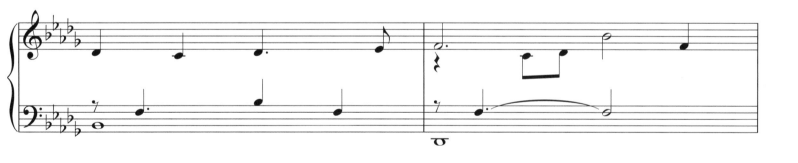

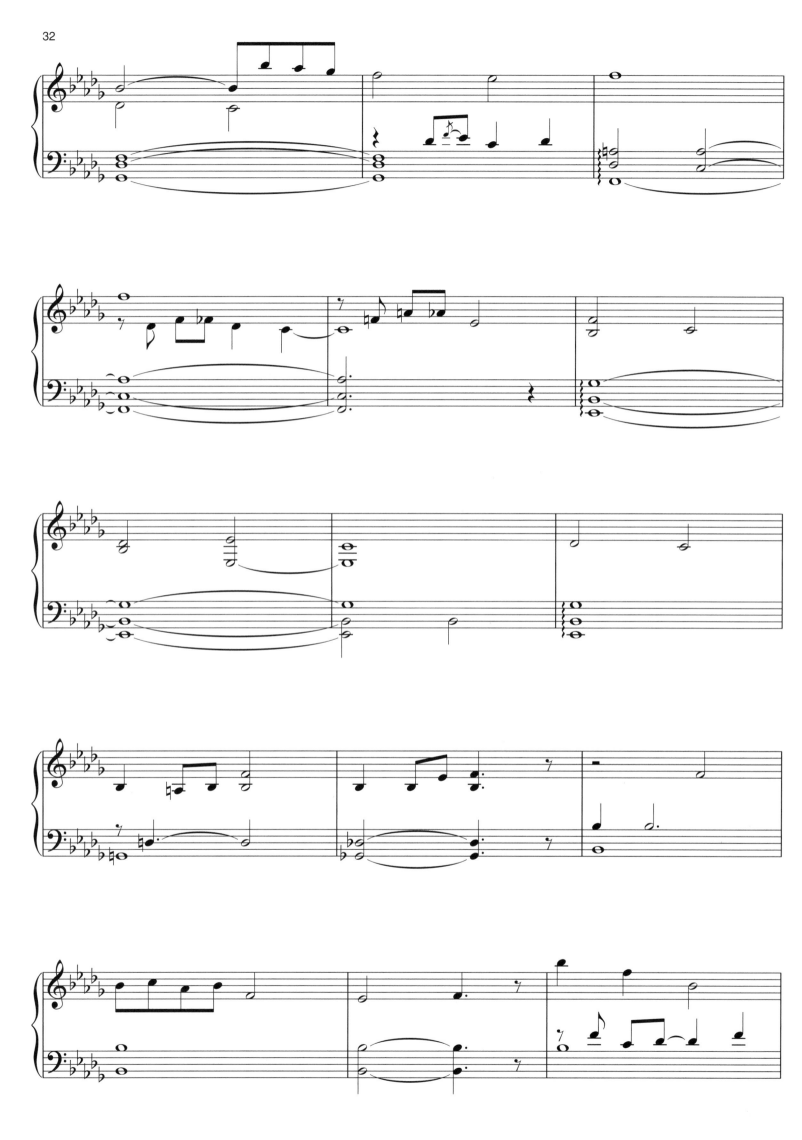

TO VOLTERRA

Composed by ALEXANDRE DESPLAT

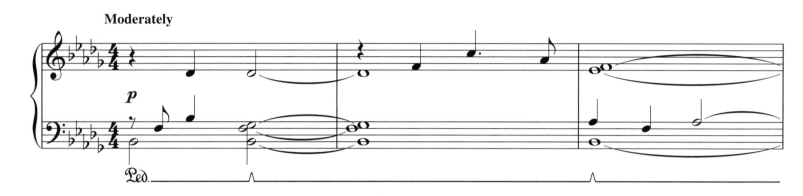

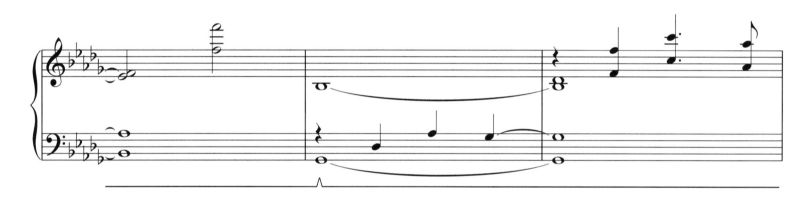

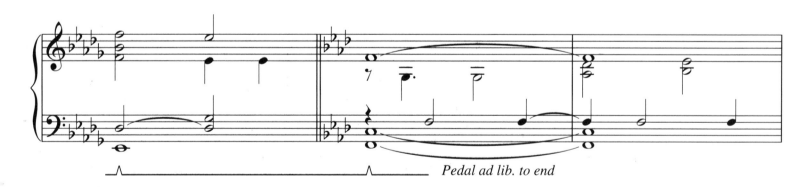

Pedal ad lib. to end

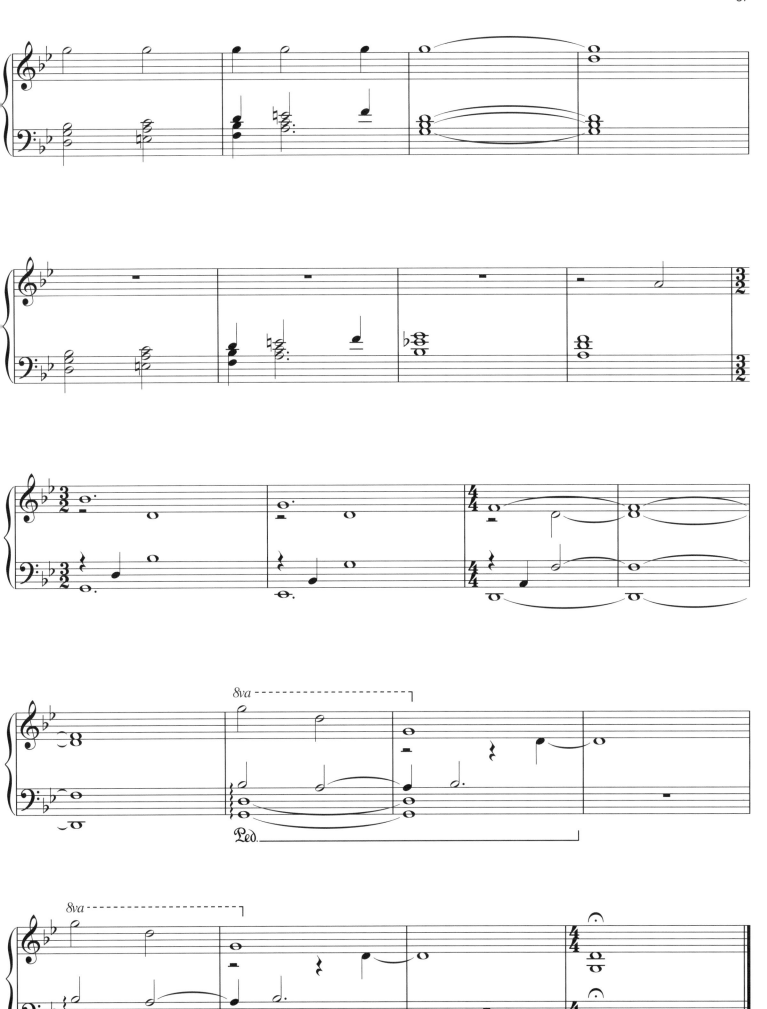

YOU'RE ALIVE

Composed by ALEXANDRE DESPLAT

Moderately slow

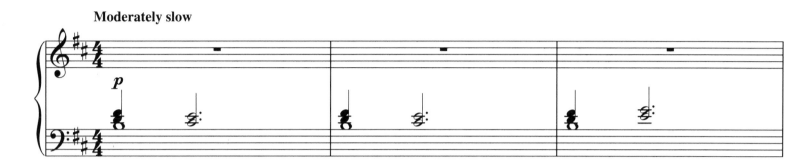

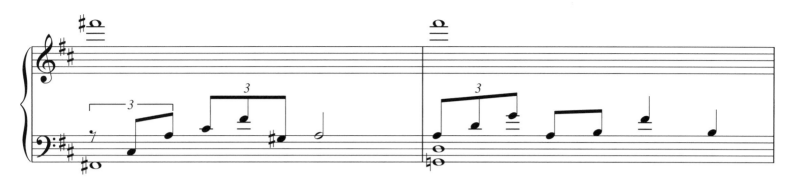

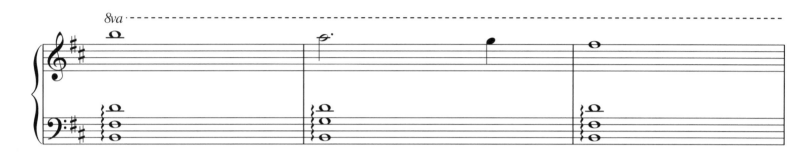

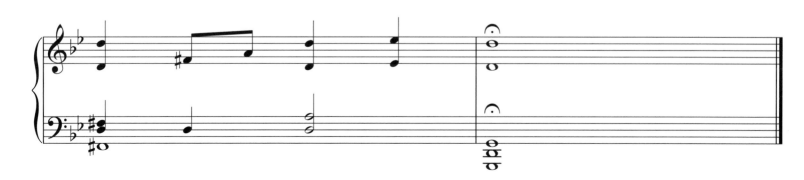

THE CULLENS

Composed by ALEXANDER DESPLAT

Moderately slow, expressively

Pedal ad lib. throughout

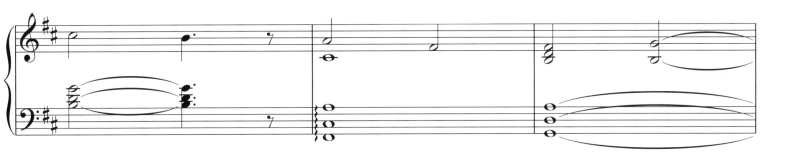

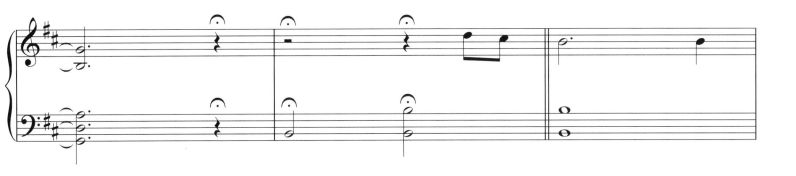

MARRY ME, BELLA

Composed by ALEXANDRE DESPLAT

Moderately

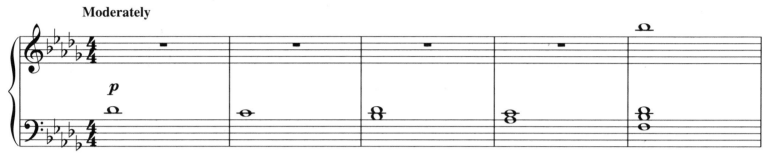

Pedal ad lib. throughout

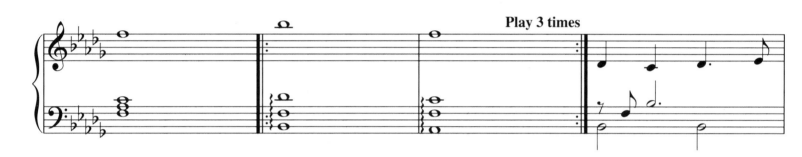

Play 3 times

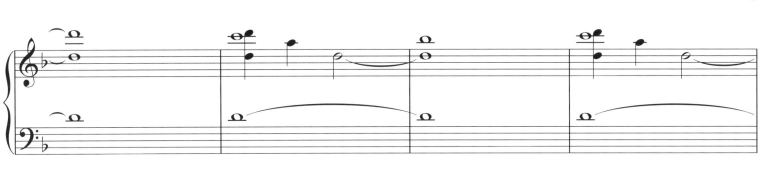

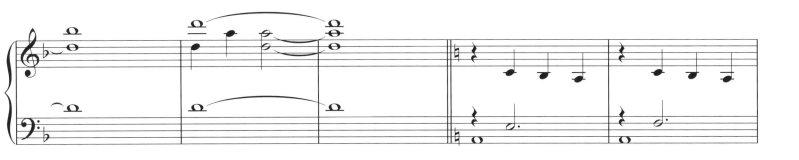

FULL MOON

Composed by ALEXANDRE DESPLAT

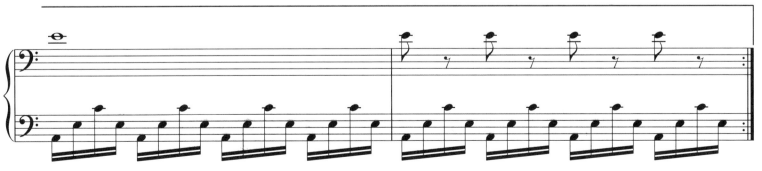